JOB DISCOVERY

JOBS IF YOU LIKE THE CREATIVE ARTS

by Kari Cornell

BrightPoint Press

San Diego, CA

an imprint of ReferencePoint Press, Inc.
Printed in the United States

For more information, contact:
BrightPoint Press
PO Box 27779
San Diego, CA 92198
www.BrightPointPress.com

LIBRARY OF CONGRESS CATALOGING-IN-PUBLICATION DATA

Names: Cornell, Kari A., author.
Title: Jobs if you like the creative arts / by Kari Cornell.
Description: San Diego, CA: BrightPoint Press, [2025] | Series: Job discovery | Includes bibliographical references and index. | Audience: Grades 7-9
Identifiers: LCCN 2024001072 (print) | LCCN 2024001073 (eBook) | ISBN 9781678209223 (hardcover) | ISBN 9781678209230 (eBook)
Subjects: LCSH: Cultural industries--Vocational guidance--Juvenile literature. | Arts--Vocational guidance--Juvenile literature.
Classification: LCC HD9999.C9472 C67 2025 (print) | LCC HD9999.C9472 (eBook) | DDC 700.23--dc23/eng/20240131
LC record available at https://lccn.loc.gov/2024001072
LC eBook record available at https://lccn.loc.gov/2024001073

CONTENTS

THE CREATIVE ARTS INDUSTRY AT A GLANCE

THE CREATIVE PROCESS

1. PREPARATION

Brainstorming Stage.
Initial idea to answer question.

2. INCUBATION

Simmering Stage.
Let the idea rest.

3. ILLUMINATION

Lightbulb Stage.
The answer for how to create the initial idea.

4. EVALUATION

Questioning Stage.
Does the answer solve the original question?

5. VERIFICATION

Creative Stage.
Artwork takes shape.

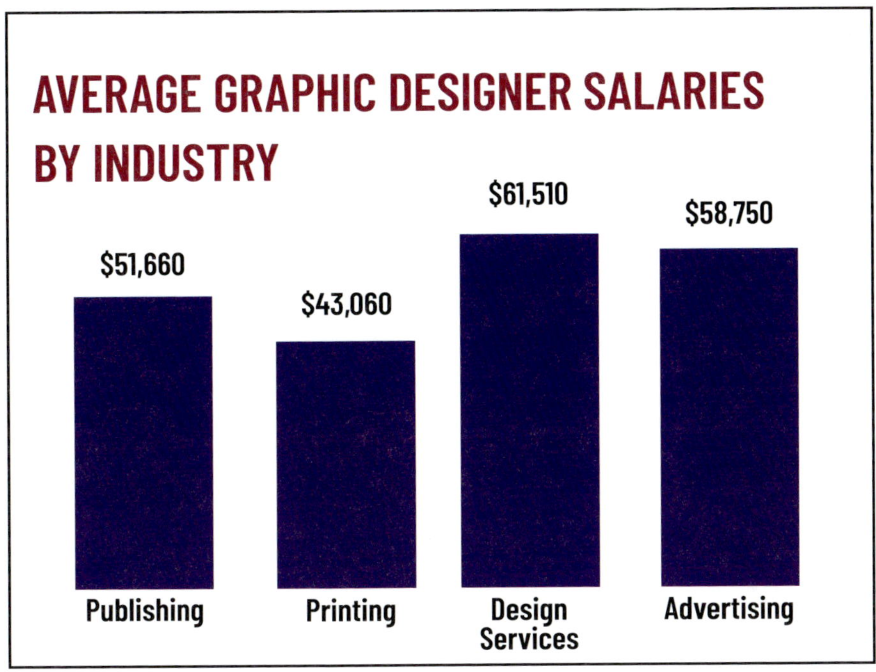

Source: "Occupational Outlook Handbook," Bureau of Labor Statistics, *September 6, 2023. bls.gov.*

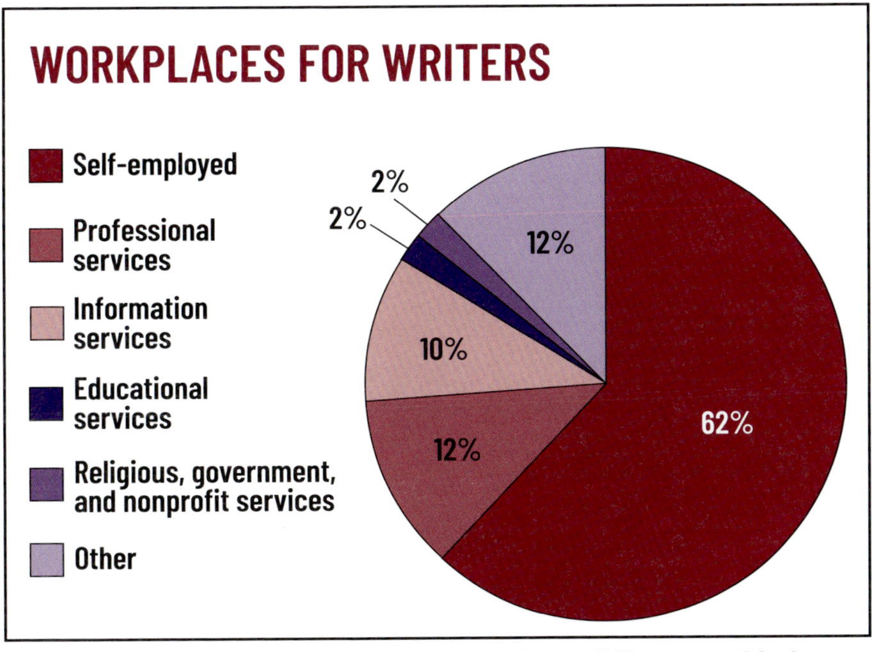

Source: "Occupational Outlook Handbook," Bureau of Labor Statistics, *September 6, 2023. bls.gov.*

WHAT IS THE CREATIVE ARTS INDUSTRY?

A man lies on a couch in his studio. He has a long gray beard. He's barefoot and wearing dark shorts and a T-shirt. The man's eyes are closed. He looks like he's napping. But that can't be possible. Loud music fills the room.

The man is Rick Rubin, and he's not sleeping. He's working. Rubin is focusing on the music. He's listening to the guitar riff. He hears when the drums gradually

Famed music producer Rick Rubin has helped shape the sound of many popular artists.

Producers play a key role in the process of making music.

grow louder. "I try to listen as closely as I possibly can," he explains. "And when my eyes are closed, I feel like I'm there with the music."[1]

Rubin is a music producer. He's produced hit songs for stars such as Johnny Cash, Lana Del Ray, and Lady Gaga. He started recording music in college in 1982.

Producing music involves more than just listening. Rubin hires musicians to play on the **tracks**. He may suggest which songs to record. He also helps musicians solve problems. Pop singer Kesha explains, "I was writing a song and I couldn't articulate what I needed to say. And he was like, 'Go home and write a full essay about everything you need to say until you can't write anymore.' And then the song kinda started forming itself."[2] Rubin has become one of today's top music producers.

THE BUSINESS OF CREATIVITY

Music production is a career in the creative arts industry. People in this industry use the creative process to make something new. They create music, books, movies, games, and more. They also design beautiful spaces for living or working.

CHAPTER ONE

MUSIC PRODUCER

Music producer may be the perfect career for music lovers. Producers make important decisions for music recordings. They come up with a vision for the mood and tone. They decide which songs to include on an album. They hire musicians and rent a recording studio. They oversee a creative team of sound engineers, songwriters, and artists.

Music producers get to listen to music at work, but the job includes much more than that.

Most importantly, producers make artists feel excited about creating music. Mark Ronson has produced records for

Music Producer

Education: 2-year degree in music production or 4-year degree in music, music theory, or fine arts

Personal Qualities: A fan of making and listening to music, creative, innovative, a good communicator, confident, knowledgeable about audio engineering

Certification and Licensing: Not required, but certification in music production, audio arts, or talent management can be an advantage

Working Conditions: Music producers may work in a professional recording studio or a home studio. The work is creative, fast-paced, and collaborative.

Average Salary: $49,246

Adele and Paul McCartney. “You have to almost be a coach, in a way,” Ronson says. “You have to make them feel like they’re incredible so that when they go in the booth to record the guitar, the vocals, or whatever it is, they really feel like they are larger than life.”[3]

Producers use mixing and mastering to shape the music. During a recording, each element of a song is recorded in a single track. Guitar, drums, and vocals each have a track. Mixing puts all the tracks together. Then producers adjust each track so they sound good together. Mastering is like putting a frame around a painting. It refines the song and makes it sound better overall.

Producers may also make creative decisions with the artist. They may

compose songs themselves. They may help promote the artist. Not every music producer does all of these things. But these skills can be part of the job.

TRAINING AND SKILLS

There is more than one path to becoming a music producer. Some producers don't have formal training. But for most, a 2-year or 4-year degree is the first step. Students learn about music theory. Music theory involves topics such as melody, harmony, and rhythm. Producers should understand how music works. Students also study songwriting, music **genres**, and composition. They take classes in business, marketing, and finance.

Producers work closely with musicians to craft great songs.

Producers learn to use soundboards. These devices collect the sound from multiple microphones. Controls on the boards let producers adjust each audio source.

Students can also earn certificates in music production. Certification can be attractive to employers. It shows a student's interest in the music industry. Earning a certificate can take up to 18 months.

Skill Building

Music producers love music. Many like to make music themselves. They follow the music scene closely. Those interested in producing immerse themselves in music. They listen to a wide variety of artists. They go to concerts. These experiences provide insight into making great music.

Internships can give producers experience working with professional studio equipment.

HOW TO GET STARTED

Colleges partner with companies to offer internships. These temporary jobs give students a chance to work in the industry. Internships may be at record labels or radio stations.

The music industry relies on making connections. One way to build a network

Powerful yet inexpensive equipment has opened music production to more people.

is to join professional organizations. The Association of Music Producers (AMP) is one example. These organizations offer classes, host conferences, and post job openings. Following industry leaders on social media is a great way to keep up with trends.

FUTURE DIRECTIONS

In 2022, recorded music sales soared to $15.9 billion in the United States. This was a record high. People are buying music more than ever before. This is great news for the industry.

Modern technology lets independent artists produce their own music. A laptop computer, music software, and an **audio interface** are needed. A microphone and headphones let an artist record and hear the music. Musicians can share songs using social media. Online music stores give musicians a way to earn money. One of the most popular is Bandcamp. More new music is available to listeners every day.

The technology for making music continues to advance. Music producers need to stay updated on these developments. People in the music industry must constantly adapt and learn.

FIND OUT MORE

Association of Music Producers (AMP)
www.associationofmusicproducers.org
The website for the AMP includes information about events and awards for the music production industry.

National Association for Recording Industry Professionals (NAIRP)
www.narip.com
The NARIP is a resource for jobs in the industry, educational opportunities, and a mentorship program.

CHAPTER TWO

GRAPHIC DESIGNER

The work of graphic designers is everywhere. It is on cereal boxes, billboards, and store signs. Graphic designers create packages, ads, books, and more. To do this, they combine words, photos, colors, and shapes. Their designs are meant to share ideas, convince, or inspire. Ads convince people to do or buy something. Book cover designs inspire people to read the book.

Graphic designers work with clients to create memorable, attractive designs.

Graphic Designer

Education: 2-year or 4-year degree

Personal Qualities: Creative, tech savvy, a good communicator, analytical, able to manage time wisely, flexible, well-versed in design principles

Certification and Licensing: Not required, but there are certification programs in graphic design, UX design, and design software

Working Conditions: Graphic designers generally work in an office. Designers working at companies may work alongside other designers. Freelancers may work from a home office.

Average Salary: $50,710

Number of Jobs: 265,000 (2021)

Future Job Outlook: 3 percent increase in jobs predicted between 2022 and 2032

Graphic designers usually specialize in a type of design. A package designer makes eye-catching packaging for products. An advertising designer creates print or digital ads. A logo designer makes images that represent a company **brand**. A designer in the publishing field makes books or magazines.

TRAINING AND SKILLS

Most graphic designers earn a degree in graphic design or fine arts. This may be a 2-year or 4-year degree. In these programs, people study the principles of design. These are guidelines designers use when they work. They include balance, pattern, and variety. Design students also take studio art classes such as drawing and painting.

They learn how to design on the computer. Students also learn about how books and magazines are printed. They study how to design websites. Design students may take classes in writing, marketing, and business.

Learning to use design software, such as Adobe Photoshop, is vital for graphic designers.

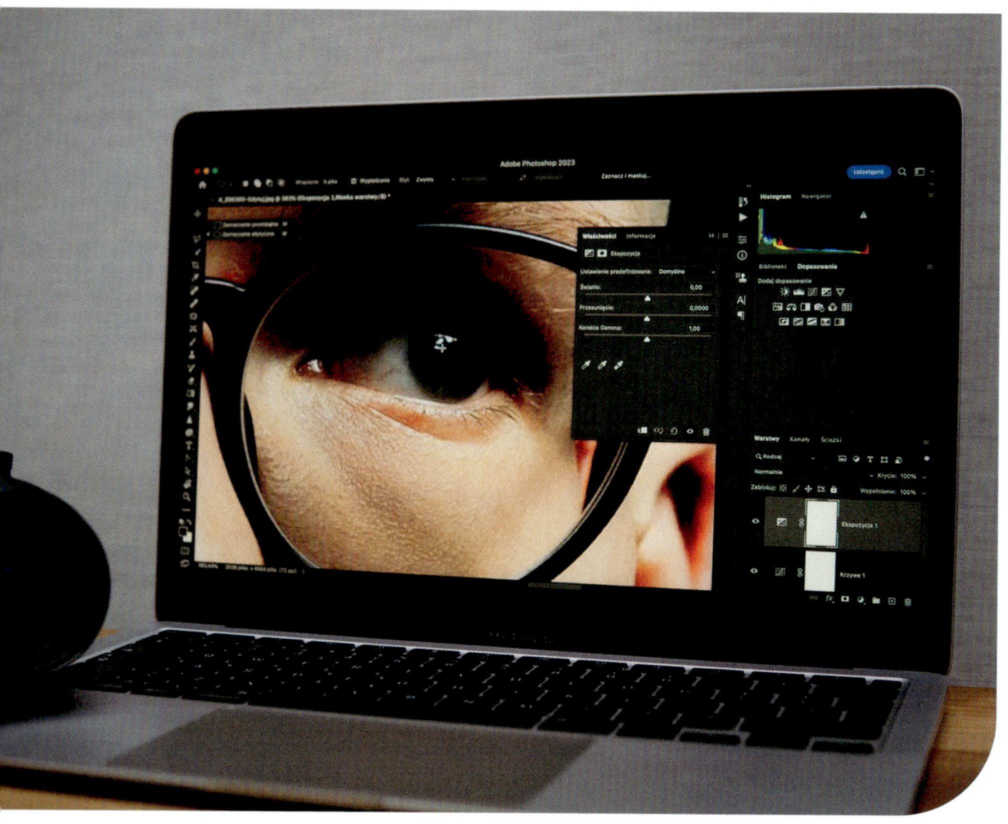

Designers might sketch their ideas on paper. But most graphic design work is done on computers. Designers learn how to use software such as Adobe Photoshop, Adobe Illustrator, and Adobe InDesign. With Photoshop, designers can edit photos. Illustrator is a digital drawing program. Images created in these two programs

Paula Scher

New York–based Paula Scher is an influential graphic designer. She designs subway posters, signs for museums, and building interiors. Scher says, "I love working on projects with a lot of possibilities that afford me the opportunities to make something more unusual."

Quoted in Julia Gamolina, "A Life in Her Work: Pentagram's Paula Scher on Ideas, Invention, and Learning," Madame Architect, *July 27, 2020, www.madamearchitect.com.*

can be brought into InDesign. InDesign allows designers to combine text and images to create page layouts. Companies other than Adobe make similar programs. Design software changes with technology. Designers must take classes to stay up to date.

HOW TO GET STARTED

Graphic design students should create a portfolio. This is a collection of their design projects. It showcases the designer's creativity and skills. Portfolios may be posted online so they can be easily shared.

Graphic design students often do an internship before graduating. Internships let students see what the design process is like. Interns experience being part of a

Working alongside experienced designers can help students learn about the field of graphic design.

design team. Sometimes internships lead to a job offer.

Making connections in the field is important. Students can meet people through professional organizations. These include the American Institute of Graphic Artists (AIGA) and the Graphic Artists Guild.

Members can learn about design trends, job opportunities, and conferences.

FUTURE DIRECTIONS

The field of graphic design is changing. Jobs designing for newspapers, magazines, or book publishers are declining. But more online designers are needed. Graphic designers have many skills that transfer to other design jobs. For example, user experience (UX) designers help create apps or websites. They focus on making these things easy to use.

The future of graphic design includes artificial intelligence (AI). AI technologies like Adobe Sensei can help designers get more done. The program automates repetitive tasks such as cropping photos.

AI systems offer designers another tool to help them work more efficiently.

Graphic design is not a skill that can be handed over to AI. Zaheer Dodhia is the CEO of Logo Design. He explains, "To date, we haven't come across AI designers that can adapt . . . cultural nuances in designs. . . . Human graphic designers are needed to facilitate the understanding of more abstract concepts."[4] Designers with the ability to adapt to new technologies will thrive.

FIND OUT MORE

American Institute of Graphic Arts (AIGA)
www.aiga.org
AIGA is the oldest and largest professional organization for graphic designers. It promotes professional development through classes and seminars.

Graphic Artists Guild
www.graphicartistsguild.org
The Graphic Artists Guild offers graphic designers the tools they need to craft a successful career. It provides resources and holds social events and classes.

CHAPTER THREE

INTERIOR DESIGNER

Interior designers create living spaces that are comfortable and beautiful. Designers must consider the building's location. They also think about how the space will be used. Interior designers balance creative and technical elements. Their goal is to design spaces that improve people's lives.

Interior designers work with a creative team. A lead designer is in charge. An interior design assistant helps the

Interior designers select colors, materials, and floorplans to fit their clients' needs.

Interior Designer

Education: 2-year or 4-year degree in interior design

Personal Qualities: Creative, able to predict trends, a good communicator, able to sketch, tech savvy, a good problem solver, able to visualize ideas, good at research

Certification and Licensing: National Council for Interior Design Qualification (NCIDQ) required in many states

Working Conditions: Interior designers work in offices at design, architectural, or engineering companies. They also meet with clients on-site to study the space and environment.

Average Salary: $61,590

Number of Jobs: 94,900 (2022)

Future Job Outlook: 4 percent increase in jobs predicted between 2022 and 2032

lead designer. The assistant handles schedules and budgets. Interior decorators design the look of a room. They choose furniture, colors, and decorations.

TRAINING AND SKILLS

Interior designers must have a degree from an **accredited** interior design program. A 2-year degree is the minimum requirement. A 4-year degree gives students more career options. Students may choose to specialize in homes, businesses, or restaurants. Other areas include health care, hotels, and schools.

Students study interior design, drawing, and **computer-aided design (CAD)**. They learn about color theory. This is the art of using color in appealing ways.

Group projects give interior design students a chance to sharpen their skills and practice working with others.

Students practice using software to make a 3D model of a space. Designers must learn about using different materials. They study the history of construction. They learn about building codes. These are rules designed to make buildings safe. They also study sustainable building design. This means making buildings with a low environmental impact.

After graduation, people must take a test to get a design license. This test is called the National Council for Interior Design Qualification (NCIDQ). In 2023, twenty-eight states required interior designers to earn this certification. Interior designers may decide to earn more certifications. Many design firms look for employees who are LEED certified. This means Leadership in Energy and Environmental Design. These are guidelines for designing energy-efficient buildings.

HOW TO GET STARTED

Students can learn about interior design careers by doing an internship. Internships might be in the student's preferred area of design. But those focused on other areas can be useful as well. Some design schools have mentorship programs. Students are teamed with an interior designer. They shadow the mentor. Students can ask mentors about their work. Students should

Many companies and organizations want building designs that meet environmental standards.

also make connections in the field. Joining professional organizations is one way to do this.

Interior design students must create a strong portfolio. It may include paid work or work from internships. It may also feature student work or side projects. Pieces should show the student's knowledge. The portfolio should tell the story of each project. This includes details about the client's request. It may describe the project's goals and challenges.

FUTURE DIRECTIONS

Projected growth in interior design is limited over the next decade. Competition for these jobs will be strong. Designers must work hard to set themselves apart.

An interior designer's portfolio might show that they specialize in simple, modern spaces.

Technology will continue to impact interior design. Online platforms such as Pinterest show off beautiful interior spaces. Many people are inspired to update their own homes. This opens up opportunities for designers. Designer David Kleinberg says, "We've seen an expansion of creative people working at a small scale. . . . That kind of craftsmanship will become even more prized."[5]

Virtual Reality Designs

Interior designers work in real-life 3D spaces. Using virtual reality (VR) to present design ideas is an appealing option. Designers can use a computer to create a 3D model of a room. The client can wear a VR headset to explore the space.

Advanced technology allows designers to visualize spaces on their computers before building them in real life.

Social media will continue to be a place for designers to showcase their work. In the future, more people will create video tours of their designs. They may even create digital 3D models for their portfolios.

FIND OUT MORE

American Society of Interior Designers (ASID)

www.asid.org

ASID provides career guidance and training for interior designers.

International Interior Design Association (IIDA)

www.iida.org

IIDA is a community for the design industry. It has members from around the world. It offers mentorship and education opportunities.

CHAPTER FOUR

WRITER

Walter Mosley is a novelist. He gives this advice to writers: "If you want to be a writer, you have to write every day."[6] Writing every day is not as hard as it might sound. Especially since writing isn't limited to novels.

Writers create content for all types of media. Novelists write fiction books. Journalists write articles for newspapers. Copywriters develop text for websites.

Writers can do their work almost anywhere.

Writer

Education: 4-year degree in English, Communications, or Journalism

Personal Qualities: Creative, a fan of reading, curious, a strong researcher, observant, detail oriented, disciplined, good with words

Certification and Licensing: Certifications for certain types of writing, such as Certified Grant Writer, are available but not required

Working Conditions: Many writers work for companies in an office. Others work or freelance from a home office. Writers spend long hours in front of a computer screen, writing or researching.

Average Salary: $73,150

Number of Jobs: 151,200 (2022)

Future Job Outlook: 4 percent increase in jobs predicted between 2022 and 2032

Screenwriters write scripts for movies and TV shows. Grant writers apply for funding for their nonprofit organizations. Technical writers create clear instructions.

Writers often focus on a particular subject. They research using sources and interviews. They create an outline. They use the outline as a road map for their story. They write a rough draft. They edit the text to make the ideas easier to understand. The writer then works with an editor. The editor helps revise the writing for publication.

TRAINING AND SKILLS

Writers usually go to college to earn 4-year degrees in English, journalism, or communications. They take classes in the English language, literature, and creative writing. Journalism students study reporting and editing. More specific classes may cover topics such as magazine writing

College writing classes give students a chance to review and discuss each other's work.

or online journalism. Communications majors take classes in writing, media strategies, and art direction.

Writers with technical experience have an advantage. Digital media companies seek out writers with computer skills. Those who can create a visual story with video will also stand out.

HOW TO GET STARTED

Many college writing departments partner with media companies to provide

Read to Write

Writers can get better by reading. For writers, reading is a form of research. They read many books and articles written in all types of styles. This teaches them how to tell stories and use language. It can help them find their own voice.

internships. Students often get college credit for completing internships. Interns write stories and do research. They may also conduct interviews. These tasks give new writers a chance to learn the publishing process. Young writers can make connections in the field. Sometimes interns receive job offers.

Writers may also join professional organizations. Groups such as the Writers Guild Foundation provide a community for writers. These groups provide access to training sessions and job opportunities.

Building a portfolio is important for writers as well. Potential employers may ask to see samples of a writer's work. A portfolio might include work completed during internships or classes. Work created

Consistently writing and building up a portfolio of work can help writers impress potential clients.

for freelance clients can also be a great addition to a portfolio.

FUTURE DIRECTIONS

The future of writing is digital. According to a 2020 Pew Research Center survey,

ChatGPT and similar AI tools are likely to change the way many writers work.

86 percent of Americans get their news online. And Americans spend about 7 hours of each day consuming online content. Digital content needs to be short and catchy. It must be formatted in an appealing way. Skills in search engine optimization (SEO) are useful. SEO involves using keywords to make web pages show up in online search results.

Many people think artificial intelligence (AI) is a threat to writers. AI includes many types of software. Among the best-known are large language models (LLMs). An LLM studies vast amounts of writing. It then writes text on its own, using statistics to figure out which word is likely to come next. The results can be surprisingly humanlike. GPT-4 is one of the most popular LLMs.

Some people worry that LLMs will replace writers. But writers can also use this software as a helpful tool. For example, it can write repetitive content such as real estate listings. This frees up time for writers to focus on more thoughtful pieces. AI writing tools can also help writers come up with ideas. They can help writers be more creative and efficient.

FIND OUT MORE

The Authors Guild

www.authorsguild.org

The Author's Guild is the largest professional organization for writers. The guild supports writers by providing a sense of community. The group also advocates for author rights, fair contracts, and decent pay.

PEN America

www.pen.org

PEN America supports writers, celebrates creative expression, and defends civil liberties.

OTHER JOBS IN THE CREATIVE ARTS INDUSTRY

Potter

Potters design and make items using clay. Some potters make bowls, mugs, or plates that are used every day. Others make art for decoration. Potters must know how to run a business. Learning how to market their work is an important part of their job. Potters sell their products at craft fairs, studios, and online stores.

Animator

Animators bring cartoon and movie characters to life on screen. They create a series of drawings called frames. When these frames are shown one after another, it looks like the characters are moving. Animators may draw the characters by hand. They may also draw scenes using computer software. Animators' work may appear in movies, TV shows, or web videos.

Fashion Designer

Fashion designers come up with ideas for new clothing, shoes, and accessories. They study trends. They select fabrics and patterns. They sketch their ideas on paper. Later they create the designs using CAD programs. They work with other designers to make samples of the designs. Fashion designers present their work at fashion shows.

Game Designer

Video game designers work on a team to create new video games. They dream up game ideas, characters, and storylines. They also think of objectives. They create levels and settings for players to meet those objectives. Designers develop ideas using storyboards and flowcharts. These are visual maps of how the game is played. Designers also build and test game prototypes.

GLOSSARY

accredited

officially recognized as a quality program

audio interface

equipment that translates sounds from a microphone or instrument into a format that recording software can recognize

brand

a graphic look that represents a single company

compose

to write music

computer-aided design (CAD)

software that helps users create 2D or 3D models of products or buildings

genres

types of music, literature, or art that are defined by their style, form, or content

track

a piece of recorded music

SOURCE NOTES

INTRODUCTION: WHAT IS THE CREATIVE ARTS INDUSTRY?

1. Quoted in Anderson Cooper, "In Shangri-La with Music Producer Rick Rubin," *60 Minutes*, May 28, 2023. www.cbsnews.com.

2. Quoted in Cooper, "In Shangri-La with Music Producer Rick Rubin."

CHAPTER ONE: MUSIC PRODUCER

3. Quoted in "Mark Ronson: 'I'm Very Aware of My Place in Music,'" *The Talks*, n.d. www.the-talks.com.

CHAPTER TWO: GRAPHIC DESIGNER

4. Quoted in Zaheer Dodhia, "Will the Demand for Graphic Designers Diminish in the Near Future?," *Forbes*, October 26, 2021. www.forbes.com.

CHAPTER THREE: INTERIOR DESIGNER

5. Quoted in Tim McKeough, "What Will the Interior Design Profession Look Like 10 Years in the Future?," *Architectural Digest*, April 2, 2019. www.architecturaldigest.com.

CHAPTER FOUR: WRITER

6. Quoted in Walter Mosely, "For Authors, Fragile Ideas Need Loving Every Day," *New York Times*, July 3, 2000. www.archive.nytimes.com.

INDEX

IMAGE CREDITS

Cover: © VH-Studio/Shutterstock Images
4: © Victor/Digital Vision Vectors/iStockphoto
5: © Red Line Editorial
7: © Kathy Hutchins/Shutterstock Images
8: © Gorodenkoff/Shutterstock Images
11: © PeopleImages.com-Yuri A/Shutterstock Images
15: © santypan/Shutterstock Images
17: © Metech Multimedia/Shutterstock Images
18: © anon_tae/Shutterstock Images
23: © Pixel-Shot/Shutterstock Images
26: © Kamil Zajaczkowski/Shutterstock Images
29: © Robert Kneschke/Shutterstock Images
31: © Gorodenkoff/Shutterstock Images
35: © CandyBox Images/Shutterstock Images
38: © goodluz/Shutterstock Images
40: © David Tran Photo/Shutterstock Images
42: © Gabi Moisa/Shutterstock Images
44: © Gorodenkoff/Shutterstock Images
47: © ZoFot/Shutterstock Images
50: © Jacob Lund/Shutterstock Images
53: © ZoFot/Shutterstock Images
54: © Valiantsin Suprunovich/Shutterstock Images
58 (top): © mavo/Shutterstock Images
58 (bottom): © SeventyFour/Shutterstock Images
59 (top): © Amnaj Khetsamtip/Shutterstock Images
59 (bottom): © DC Studio/Shutterstock Images

ABOUT THE AUTHOR

Kari Cornell is an award-winning children's book author who gardens, runs, and makes pottery. She lives in Minneapolis with her husband, their two boys, and their sweet dog, EmmyLou.